T0150822

WHAT I LOVE ABOUT YOU

Best Friend

WHAT I LOVE ABOUT YOU
Best Friend

**A BOOK TO
PERSONALISE
FOR SOMEONE
YOU LOVE**

A STUDIO PRESS BOOK

First published in the UK in 2021 by Studio Press,
an imprint of Bonnier Books UK
4th Floor, Victoria House
Bloomsbury Square, London WC1B 4DA
Owned by Bonnier Books
Sveavägen 56, Stockholm, Sweden
www.bonnierbooks.co.uk

3 5 7 9 10 8 6 4 2

ISBN 978-1-80078-146-7

Originally published in German by riva Verlag,
an imprint of Münchner Verlagsgruppe GmbH in 2017

A CIP catalogue for this book is available from the British Library
Printed and bound in Italy

You can live without many things – but your best friend isn't one of them. They're unique, impossible to live without and irreplaceable. They're the sibling you'd have chosen yourself, a gift from above and one of your favourite people in the whole world.

A best friend understands you when you don't really understand yourself. They'll be there for you, any time of the day or night, in any corner of the world, just to give you what you need the most: comfort, tissues, chocolate or a few encouraging words to tell you that that idiot really isn't worth it. They're a kick up the rear when you need it and the voice of reason. Nevertheless, just the smallest glance is enough for you both to burst into hysterical laughter. When they're by your side, life is easier and pain more bearable. Obviously, other people think you're absolutely crazy. But that's what makes your friendship special.

It's time to pay homage to and celebrate your friend, because they're more than a friend. They're THE BEST FRIEND IN THE WORLD.

———O———

My dear .... ,
This book is a personal declaration of friendship
for you and is full of things that I find absolutely
amazing about you and us. No one is like you,
and I have no idea how I would get along
without you.
Yours,

....

———O———

This is us – stunning, distinct and inseparable – a pair like:

☐ Fire and brimstone   ☐ Salt and pepper

☐ Beginning and end   ☐ Yin and yang

We've known each other for .... years!

The happy day we met was:

We were here:

....

These people were with us:

....

....

My first impression of you was:

....

....

....

And this is what I immediately found so nice about you:

....

....

I thought:

☐ We were going to become a fabulous duo

☐ We'd never, ever become friends

This was one of our first adventures together:

....

....

....

....

Do you remember?

You did this and I found it quite impressive:

....

....

....

And I was shocked by:

....

....

....

....

An object, an item of clothing or something else of yours
that you always used to carry around with you:

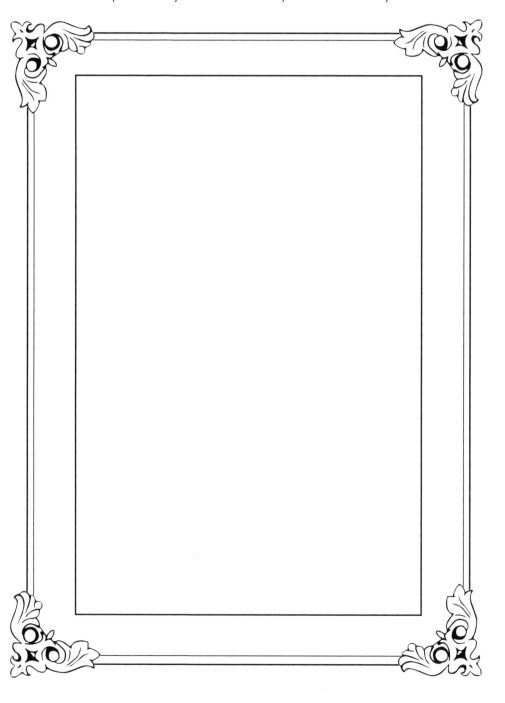

Before I got to know you better, I thought this about you:

☐ You're really nice   ☐ You're really weird

You lived here when I first met you:

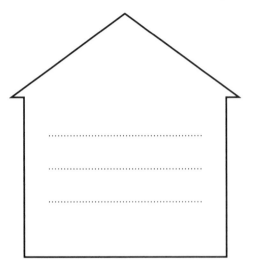

And I lived here:

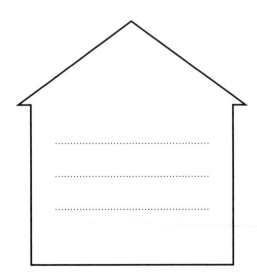

This brought us closer together:

....

....

....

....

Our best shopping trip to date is:

....

....

....

....

Everything we bought:

When I talk about you to others, I call you this:

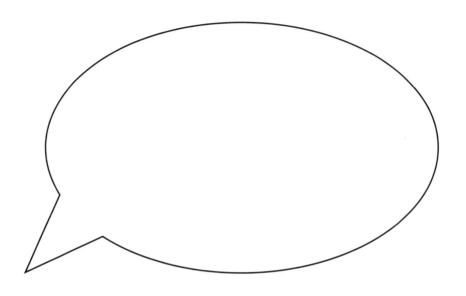

Only you're allowed to call me: ....

I remember how we once:

....

....

....

....

....

....

....

I have to smile when I think back.

I love it when you pull this face:

And I love it when you say:

....

....

Our favourite drink:

Can we please swap this body part?

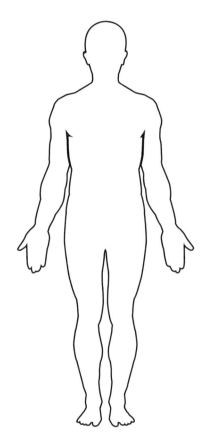

When I'm with you, I'm much:

- ☐ Cooler
- ☐ More confident
- ☐ Braver
- ☐ Sillier

- ☐ More relaxed
- ☐ Happier
- ☐ Crazier
- ☐ ....

This is the first photo of us together that I could find:

My three favourite qualities of yours:

- ....
- ....
- ....

I love to do these things with you:

☐ Cook fancy food   ☐ Laze about in the sun

☐ Watch action-packed films   ☐ Go from one bar to the next

☐ Go window shopping   ☐ People-watch

Exactly this much of my heart belongs to you:

With no one else can I do the following as well as I can with you:

☐ Have a good moan   ☐ Chill

☐ Chat   ☐ Party

If necessary, I'd travel here for you:

....

If I had a big pile of money,
I'd buy this for you:

When you phone me:

☐ I'm in a better mood
straight away

☐ I always have a laugh

☐ I never want to hang up

☐ My world is in order again

This is how you make me laugh:

....

....

....

....

....

One of the nicest things you've ever said to me is:

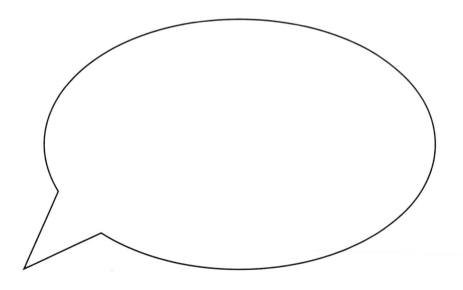

I found it great that you said this:

....

....

....

It was to this person:

....

You're:

☐ The salt in my soup   ☐ The DJ at my party

☐ The milk in my tea   ☐ The funniest person I've
                                 ever encountered

I solemnly swear that I'll never:

....

....

....

And I'll always:

....

....

....

I know you love: ....

I've tried to draw a picture of it here:

You once said something very wise:

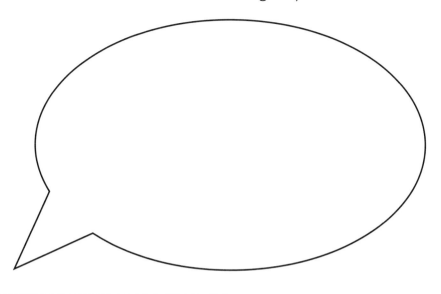

I find this great about you:

....

....

....

These things are important to me in a friendship and you fulfil each one:

- ....
- ....
- ....
- ....
- ....

If everyone was like you, the world would be more:

....

This was a very special day for us:

Because we:

....

....

....

You can do this really well:

....

....

....

....

....

....

And this, too:

....

....

....

To be honest, your choice of partner is:

☐ Spot on   ☐ Always a near miss

☐ Usually good but with   ☐ Always a total miss
   a few exceptions

Next time you completely miss the mark, I'll:

....

....

.... , I promise!

This colour suits you particularly well:

....

And I think you look really good with this hairstyle:

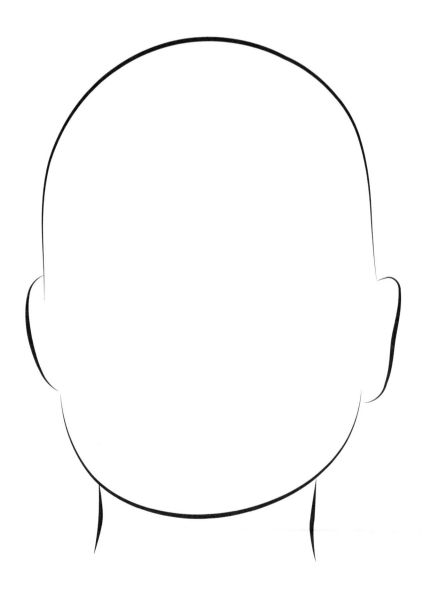

This item of clothing looks great on you:

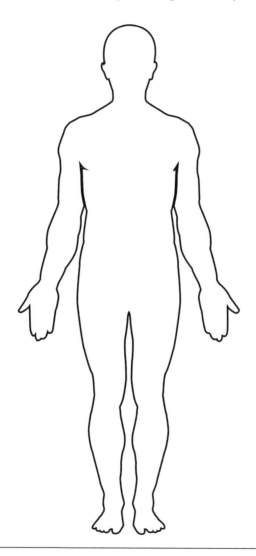

An outfit of yours I wish I had is:

....

....

....

I'm on your side, no matter which side that is.

And if: ....

does this to you again: ....

I'll hit them over the head with a baseball bat, I promise!

No matter when, no matter why, I'll always have:

☐ A bottle of gin   ☐ A hug

☐ A strong shoulder   ☐ Comfort and a pack of tissues

☐ Ice cream and chocolate   ☐ ....

... ready for you.

This is the emoticon that I send to you most often:

And I associate this emoticon with you:

You can call me any time, even at night, when:

☐ You're unhappy

☐ Something really funny has happened

☐ Something really great has happened to you

☐ You're bored

☐ You're drunk and would otherwise call your ex

☐ ....

If I had to describe our friendship in one word, it would be:

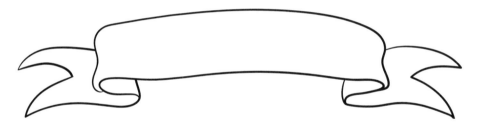

And if I had to describe you in one word, it would be:

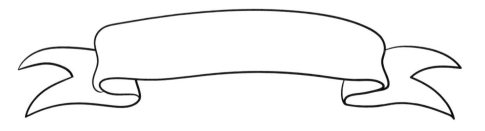

Something I can only do with you is:

....

....

I think you'd be really successful in this job:

....

Because:

....

....

....

This party was legendary:

....

....

The best thing about it was:

....

....

The nicest present you've ever given me was:

....

....

And a photo we both look great in:

Your perfect partner would be:

....

I'm sorry that I once:

....

....

....

....

Sorry

If you were an animal, you'd probably be:

....

Because:

....

....

....

When I'm at rock bottom:

☐ You pick me up again

☐ You lie next to me and don't ask me stupid questions

☐ You understand me

☐ ....

This is our song because we can
both bellow it out by heart:

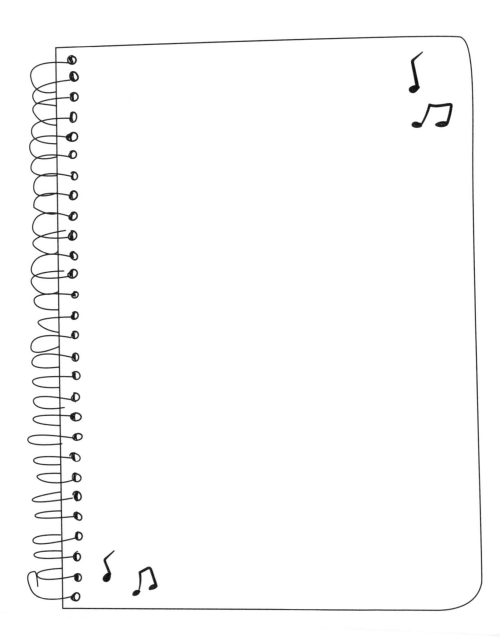

This is an adorable quirk of yours:

....

....

This is why we're unbeatable together:

....

....

....

This flower suits you best:

This kind of accessory looks great on you:

This tip from you was amazing:

....

....

....

I now do it the same way as you!

When we're both old, I imagine our friendship
will be like this:

....

....

....

....

You do this really well when dealing with others:

....

....

....

This (among other things, obviously) is what makes you so
attractive to your potential partner:

....

....

....

This is something that we can now laugh about:

....

....

....

I'll never forget what you did for me when:

....

....

....

Thanks

I'm amazed you know so much about:

....

....

I'd love to have this quality of yours:

....

....

This is a film we've watched together more times than I can count:

....

This is our favourite scene:

....

....

....

In my ideal life, you live here:

....

....

....

And I live here:

....

....

....

We'd have lots of this: ....

And we'd do this: ....

I nearly fell off my chair laughing when you told me this:

....

....

....

....

....

....

....

....

A photo of us that's absolutely hilarious:

You have particularly great taste in:

....

Why you're my best friend in one sentence:

....

....

....

We can have a really good moan about: ....

....

Ten things we both like:

☺ ....

☺ ....

☺ ....

☺ ....

☺ ....

☺ ....

☺ ....

☺ ....

☺ ....

☺ ....

Ten things neither of us like:

☹ ....

☹ ....

☹ ....

☹ ....

☹ ....

☹ ....

☹ ....

☹ ....

☹ ....

☹ ....

Do you remember flirting with this person?
They looked like this:

This was at: ....

I wouldn't even swap you for these things:

☐ All the money in the world   ☐ The perfect body

☐ A sports car   ☐ ....

I think this is our biggest similarity:

....

Thank you for trying to make me less:

....

....

And more:

....

....

Three words that you say really often:

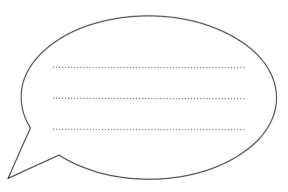

....
....
....

This is a typical phrase of yours:

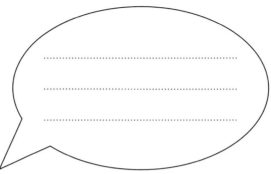

....

....

....

I was maybe a teeny, tiny bit jealous once. That was because:

....

....

....

This is a time you totally surprised me:

....

....

A really good beauty tip I've picked up from you:

....

....

....

....

If I could do your make-up, it'd look like this:

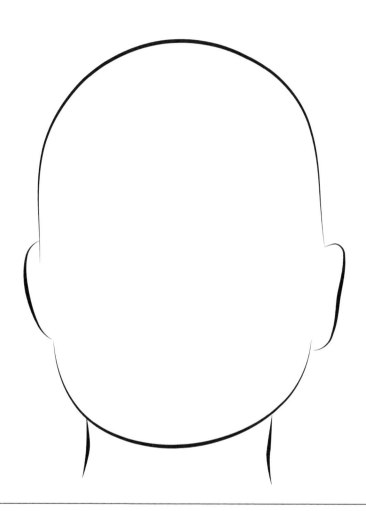

Why I go shopping with you:

☐ Because you're the best style adviser

☐ Because it's the most fun with you

☐ Because you know where the nicest things are

☐ ....

Your.. are the best!

If I could give you a lifetime supply of..,
I'd do it straight away.

What I love about our
friendship:

Something I only talk about with you:

We overcame this fight or difference in opinion really well:

....

....

When we're together: ....

Our favourite TV series:

The worst thing about it is:

....

....

....

....

And the best thing about it is:

....

....

....

....

....

Here's a recipe I'd like to cook for you:

Ingredients

- ....
- ....
- ....
- ....
- ....
- ....

Method

....
....
....
....
....
....
....
....
....

Here's an outline of my hand.
When you need me, hold it against your cheek:

Five objects that make me think of you straight away:

♥ ....

♥ ....

♥ ....

♥ ....

♥ ....

I'd do this for you, if you asked me nicely:

....

....

....

I miss you a lot when:

....

....

....

The most embarrassing thing that's ever happened to us is this:

....

....

....

....

At least we can laugh about it now.

Thankfully, no one hears us when we: .... ,
otherwise we would have long been: ....

Something we chat about together:

....

....

....

....

Something we keep quiet about:

....

....

....

....

....

I trust you .... per cent.

I'd never neglect you. Not even when:

....

....

This year, I really hope that you'll:

....

....

.... could learn a lot from you about

....!

You think you can't do this very well:

.... : ☐ That's true ☐ That's not true at all

.... : ☐ That's true ☐ That's not true at all

.... : ☐ That's true ☐ That's not true at all

I've picked up this quirk from you:

....

....

Thanks for that!

I'd even like you if you looked like this:

If you mixed our first names, we'd get this name:

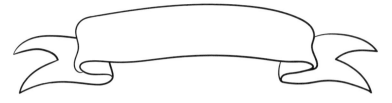

This evening was absolutely legendary:

....

....

Only we understand this inside joke:

....

....

If we were in a rock band, then we wouldn't just be
insanely cool, we'd also have the best band name.
Our band name would be:

It's unbelievable, but all of the following traits apply to you:

- [ ] Adventurous
- [ ] Breathtaking
- [ ] Sexy
- [ ] Awesome
- [ ] Charming
- [ ] Dominant
- [ ] Honest
- [ ] Elegant
- [ ] Refreshing
- [ ] Extravagant
- [ ] Fascinating
- [ ] Joyful
- [ ] Happy
- [ ] Exquisite
- [ ] Funny
- [ ] Interesting
- [ ] Powerful
- [ ] Bright
- [ ] Adorable
- [ ] Phenomenal
- [ ] Confident
- [ ] Strong
- [ ] Nice
- [ ] Amazing
- [ ] Astounding

- [ ] Wild
- [ ] Wonderful
- [ ] Reliable
- [ ] Graceful
- [ ] Athletic
- [ ] Jolly
- [ ] Special
- [ ] Great
- [ ] Brilliant
- [ ] Empathetic
- [ ] Emotional
- [ ] Surprising
- [ ] Fabulous
- [ ] Friendly
- [ ] Mysterious
- [ ] Grand
- [ ] Outstanding
- [ ] Instinctive
- [ ] Colourful
- [ ] Arty
- [ ] Endearing
- [ ] Romantic
- [ ] Sensational
- [ ] Stylish
- [ ] Dreamlike

- [ ] Incomprehensible
- [ ] Alluring
- [ ] Tentative
- [ ] High maintenance
- [ ] Attractive
- [ ] Unusual
- [ ] Admirable
- [ ] Noble
- [ ] Unique
- [ ] Delightful
- [ ] First class
- [ ] Fantastic
- [ ] Cool
- [ ] Incredible
- [ ] Uninhibited
- [ ] Pretty
- [ ] Clever
- [ ] Precious
- [ ] Lively
- [ ] Perfect
- [ ] Selfless
- [ ] Sensitive
- [ ] Turbulent
- [ ] Thoughtful
- [ ] Unbelievable

You look a bit like this celebrity:

....

I respect that you managed to do this:

....

....

....

....

....

For a perfect evening, we go here:

....

....

And drink:

....

Let's do it again soon!

You help me cope with this:

....

....

....

Thanks!

When I hold this object in my hand, I think of you:

I'd love to be able to do this as well as you:

....

....

Without you, I'd be:

☐ A great deal poorer   ☐ Probably the only silly one

☐ Half as great   ☐ ....

I'd love to delete this person from your list of friends:

....

We love to make fun of these exes:

....

....

I associate you with this book: ....

this film: ....

this number: ....

this country: ....

this place: ....

and this food: ....

So our friendship will last forever, if I meet a new partner, I swear I:

☐ Won't bring them when we have plans

☐ Won't gush about them all the time

☐ Will never speak in baby talk to them

☐ Will never tell them secrets of ours or yours

Because of you, I'm better in this way:

....

....

....

....

Thank you for always liking me even when I'm not so likeable. For example, when I:

....

....

....

....

You're like:

☐ No one else

☐ Everyone else

The Holy Booze Laws

Because I appreciate and value you, I'll…

☐ Cover your dark circles with concealer when you're too drunk

☐ Stop you from making drunk calls to your ex

☐ Hold your hair back when you're being sick

☐ Take your car keys

☐ Make sure you don't go home with some idiot

☐ Stop you from dancing naked on the tables

I sometimes worry that we might stop getting along so well or we might lose touch when:

....

....

....

....

....

It's nothing special, but we do this often and I love it:

....

....

....

....

....

This is something we could both cry our eyes out over:

....

....

....

I know you have a complete, unexplainable love for:

....

If I could, I'd send you a whole box of it!

We definitely need to go here on holiday:

....

....

And while we're on holiday we should:

....

....

....

....

....

....

I think this app was
invented just for us:

I'll defend you...

☐ From everything   ☐ Only in an emergency

☐ From anything smaller than me   ☐ Reluctantly

I don't envy you for:

....

The typical qualities of your star sign that actually
apply to you:

- ....
- ....
- ....

I'm so proud of you. This makes me particularly proud:

- ....
- ....
- ....

I remember well how you once:

....

....

I knew that you'd fall in love with:

....

This is the funniest thing you've ever said:

....

....

....

....

This is the coolest thing we've done together:

....

....

....

....

When it comes to this, I want to be a bit more like you:

....

....

....

....

This is one of my favourite snapshots of us:

If you're ever sad, think about this:

....

....

....

It'll make you laugh again, I promise!

When you're old, you'll probably be:

....

....

That'll be funny.

I hope we never stop doing this:

....

....

....

Even when we're 100 years old!

I found this ex partner of yours quite hot:

....

I've always wanted to ask you:

....

....

This is how other people can tell that we know each other really well:

....

....

I hope I'm with you at this event in your future:

....

....

And it would be really nice if you were here with me when:

....

....

I think you started this trend:

....

No matter how long it was since we last saw each other, we feel really comfortable with each other:

☐ Straight away

☐ After several long hours

☐ After five minutes

☐ ....

I like to tease you by:

....

....

But you know I'm not being mean!

I remember the face you pulled when:

....

....

And it looked something like this:

All the things you are to me:

☐ Telephone helpline   ☐ Critic

☐ Gossip buddy   ☐ Courage giver

☐ Stylist   ☐ Arse kicker

☐ Strong shoulder   ☐ Therapist

☐ Strategy adviser   ☐ Giggle partner

☐ Taste controller   ☐ Self-confidence giver

and: ....

If our friendship were a house, the foundations would be made of:

....

....

You look so happy when:

....

....

....

....

My favourite quote of yours:

We can talk about absolutely everything, even:

....

....

....

....

....

....

....

....

....

We both have this funny little habit:

....

....

If a piece of clothing didn't suit you:

☐ I wouldn't say anything so I wouldn't make you sad

☐ I'd be honest and save you from that rag

We could change the world together by:

....

....

We both laughed so hard when:

....

....

....

Things of mine you can have:

☐ My diary

☐ All my shoes

☐ My social media passwords

☐ My favourite outfit (but only borrowed)

☐ And even: ....

A picture with a very special memory:

The memory is:

....

Our favourite place to go and chat:

When we are ...., we will:

....

What I always have in the house when you come to visit:

- ....
- ....
- ....

If I could somehow persuade you, then we'd finally do this:

....

....

....

A crazy coincidence I remember:

....

....

I was really excited about this:

....

....

....

I love to borrow these items from your wardrobe:

♥ ....

♥ ....

♥ ....

On a scale from 1 to 10, you're this…

Likeable   1   2   3   4   5   6   7   8   9   10

Nice   1   2   3   4   5   6   7   8   9   10

Reliable   1   2   3   4   5   6   7   8   9   10

Funny   1   2   3   4   5   6   7   8   9   10

Good a friend   1   2   3   4   5   6   7   8   9   10

If you were reincarnated, you'd definitely be:

....

And I'd be:

....

I know you're scared of:

....

I'll protect you!

We'd better not do this any more:

....

....

If you were a superhero, you'd look like this:

I know you don't like this about yourself:

....

....

But I do.

Things we should definitely do together:

Go to this festival: ....

Take a city break here: ....

Watch this film: ....

Go dancing here: ....

Cook: ....

If we were both stranded on a desert island, we'd probably...

☐ Make a big SOS sign out of coconuts, build a camp out of palm leaves, make a fire and cook some fish

☐ Die moaning loudly on the third day after several failed attempts to find something to eat

---

If it weren't for you, I'd never have experienced this:

....

....

....

If we were to get a friendship tattoo,
it would maybe look like this:

And we'd put it here:

....

I completely trust you with these things:

....

....

....

And this is how I know you completely trust me:

....

....

....

I'd never have thought that you'd really do this:

....

....

....

Without you, my life would be:

....

....

....

....

....

My worst nightmare is you:

....

I'm so happy that you don't do this:

....

....

....

And if I had a say in it, you wouldn't do this, either:

....

....

I'd do this if I could be you for a day:

....

....

....

If you were me for a day, I hope you'd get this done for me:

....

....

....

If I randomly want to cheer you up a bit, I just have to:

....

....

Let's do this for a whole day:

....

....

I'd like to invite you to:

....
....
....

A shortlist of things we should do soon:

♥ ....

♥ ....

♥ ....

♥ ....

♥ ....

I've put together a
personalised playlist for you:

I've painted our friendship in the most beautiful colours:

This is our shopping list for a
perfect evening together:

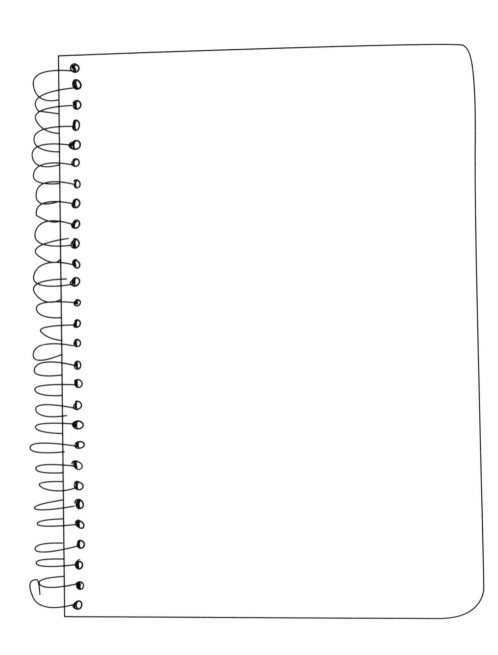

I love it when you use these swear words:

....

....

You always tell this joke:

....

....

....

....

☐ I always laugh really hard	☐ It was funny the first time
☐ I tell it myself and pretend I made it up	☐ ....

I love these things about your home:

....

....

I wish that this relation of yours was a part of my family:

....

....

I tried to draw a portrait of you:

(Please don't laugh!)

Here are some things I'd love to say to you:

Our Friendship Statistics

We've known each other this long:

☐ Months   ☐ Years

We live this many miles from each other:

☐

We phone each other this often:

☐ Never   ☐ Daily   ☐ Several times a day   ☐ Several times a month

On a scale of 1 to 10, you're this important to me:

1 2 3 4 5 6 7 8 9 10

We've been through the following together:

☐ School   ☐ Falling out   ☐ Marriage

☐ College   ☐ Making up   ☐ Having children

☐ Breaking up   ☐ Bad haircuts   ☐ ....

I'd pay this much ransom money for you:

£ ....

I'd guess your IQ to be about:

If I didn't know how old you were,
I'd say you were:

We spend most of our time:

☐ Laughing   ☐ Shopping

☐ Gossiping   ☐ Drinking coffee

☐ Relaxing   ☐ ....

Without you, I'd only be this big:

Without you, I wouldn't own these things:

♥ ....

♥ ....

♥ ....

Without you, I'd never have experienced this:

♥ ....

♥ ....

♥ ....

Without you, I'd never have achieved this:

♥ ....

♥ ....

♥ ....

Without you, I'd be:

♥ ....

♥ ....

♥ ....

With you, everything is very:

....

When you're not there:

....

You realised before me that:

....

I was worried about you when:

....

Thank you for:

....

With you by my side, I always feel:

....

I like going here with you the most:

....

When you call me:

....

I think you deserve:

....

What I wish for you:

For your future:

....

....

....

For your love life:

....

....

....

For your family:

....

....

....

For your friendships:

....

....

....

For your health:

....

....

....

For your career:

....

....

....

Finally, I've put together a collection of our silliest,
most embarrassing and best photos:

....
....
....
....

....
....
....
....

....
....
....
....

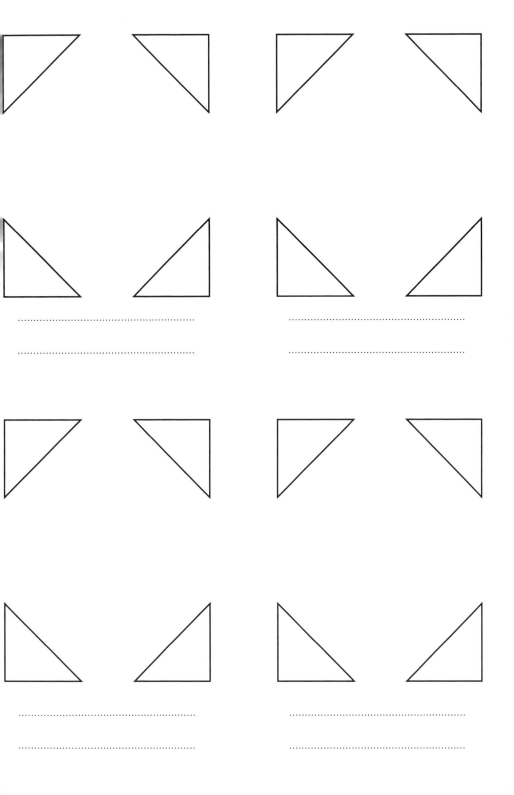

My Best Friend

There's one thing left that I'd like to say to you –
something very personal. Listen:

....

....

....

....

....

....

....

....

....

....

....

....

Yours, ...